We Must Sink
Before We Swim

Elizabeth Harper

BookLeaf Publishing

India | USA | UK

Presentation by *BookLeaf Publishing*

Web: www.bookleafpub.com

E-mail: info@bookleafpub.com

ISBN: 978-93-5761-183-1

First edition 2022

DEDICATION

To the ones who willingly watched me sink
when I could barely swim:

This collection is for you.

ACKNOWLEDGEMENT

I would like to take a moment to begin by thanking every soul who believed in the power of my voice.

Thank you to my family, friends, and fans for endlessly supporting my words. For none of this would exist without you.

PREFACE

There is a dark innocence
Inside the human mind.

Where curiosity About the
mystery of tragedy Is never
hard to find.

But the truth is…

Darkness is the foundation of salvation.

It is why we rise after we fall.

It is the meaning behind

Everything

And nothing at all.

Sink or Swim

Pain is like the sea

Deep, dark and never ending.

It will lure you in with its siren song

Then swallow you whole until your soul is gone.

And all you'll be to the sea is another sunken
ship

To house the souls that will drown in their own
misery.

I am a Masterpiece

I am a masterpiece of misery:

Each scar weaved together
To create your canvas of insanity.

And with every tear I cried
Your canvas became perfectly primed.

So each bruise of yellow, black, and blue

Would be seen as strokes of art

Painfully painted in love by you.

Like Ships that Pass in the

Night

I can't eat.
I can't sleep.

I am lost in this tragedy of you.

You were my boat when my mind was like an
anchor;
Drowning me in the dark, forbidden sea.

And you saved me

From the water And
everything that lies
Deep within its depths.

But now…

I am sinking.

I am Empty

I am empty.

Like a vase filled with dust,
But never flowers.

Alone again,

Wilting away as I cry for hours.

Empty.

Like a glass of water,

Sweating on the outside
Secretly dying to be full
One more time.

Empty.

A feeling so great,
Not even glass can escape
The immense pain
Of this emptiness I feel inside.

So how can I,

A beating heart trapped
Inside flesh and bones,

Fight this feeling of being

So incredibly alone?

Empty.

If a glass,

A material that can

withstand the heat,

Sweats and cries...

Does that mean
This emptiness
Is going to be the reason why

I finally die?

Caught Between the Devil
and the Deep Blue Sea

These tears
That formed from fears

Always

Make me slip and fall
As I'm climbing my own walls.

Crawling
On my hands and feet

Begging for someone
To bury me six feet deep.

But no one can hear my screams
About my inevitable defeat

Because these walls I've built
Are made of metal and stone.
And maybe that's why
I always feel so alone.

…But maybe one day

These walls
Will finally fall

And become the grave
I have always craved.

Maybe one day...

I won't be this way.

Like the Rain, I Fall

I am the rain

Falling down from cloudy skies
Creating wonder in children's eyes.

I am the rain

Racing across
Backseat window panes

On dark stormy nights
Illuminating the city lights.

I am the rain

Where mystery and madness
Combine as one

And fall...

Over and over again.

My Muffled Sanctuary

I dream of silence.
To dive deep into stillness.

Letting it surround me
And drown me.

Until I am at peace.

Until I am one with the void.

Until I am one

With the nothingness

That lies within the dark.

Until I become…

Silent.

I am a Prisoner

I am a prisoner.

A lost soul
To corrupt and control.

To lock away
And force to stay

Inside your chains
Of manipulation and pain.

But I know
You will never see

That you are the reason
Behind my misery.

Goodbye, Captain

Even through

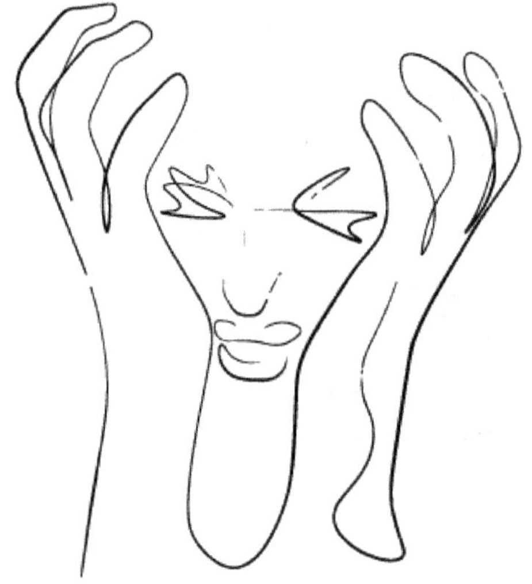

The depths of despair,

I promised I would try
To fight off the tide.

But alas,

Like my ship,

I too was doomed
To sink and die

Drowning

Through an abyss

That is the sea of your lies.

I am Drowning

I am drowning

In the sea of my own sanity.

Where the waves

Shadow the silence

To cause death and destruction.

I have fallen into their depths And
buried myself in its darkness.

Please do not dive deep to find me.

For this muffled silence is
The only way I can escape my fate.

Fuck You, I'm Great At
Yahtzee

Looking into the dark,
I felt a familiar spark.

But not just one…

Because this addiction
Will never be done

It will never be won.

The tears will fall,
And the fears will speak

Breaking you down
Until your name is "weak."

They will laugh as you cry—
All because they just want you to die.
A gun to your head,
A knife to your throat;

Only one more move
Until you start to choke.

So take a shot
And roll the dice;

Take this chance
To save your life.

12:12 am

My pain became
Liquified;

Flowing through my veins
Like the silence after rain.

Leaving my soul
Terrified.

Because without it...

I may never experience pain
The same again.

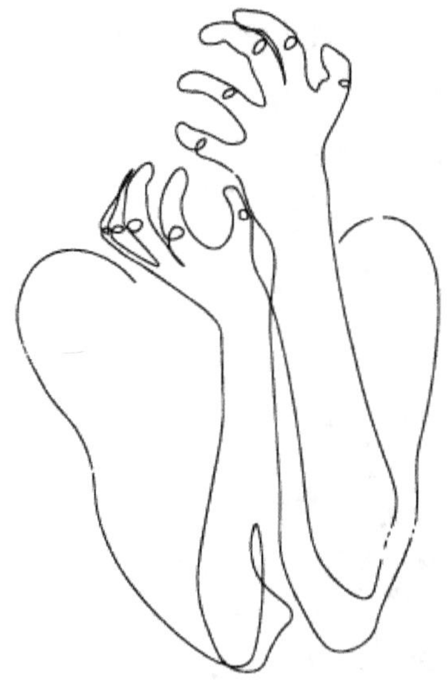

Reborn

Can these sacred waters
Heal my wounds

Like the fluid

Inside a mother's womb?

pain [pān] noun

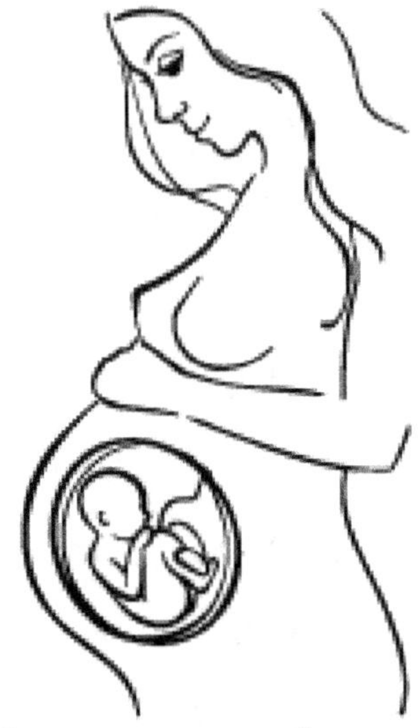

In one way or another
Pain will touch all of us.

Some will endure
The ache and mistakes;

Shining through the darkness
As they finally escape.

But some of us
Will accept our fate

Of becoming
Terrorized and traumatized

By that four-letter word
We've all come to know and hate.

12:22 pm

Pain
    Is powerful.
        Breaking…

Then
Building again.

Revelation

I am torn between
Continuing the scorn

Or becoming reborn.

The ultimate fight
Between heart and mind;

The cruel compromise
Between I and I;

The true meaning between
Death and life.

But if only a name

Then I am the torn.

I am the scorned.

And I will become

The reborn.

Batten Down the Hatches

I hate everything I was
And everything I've done.

For every word I've thought
And every lie I've sung.

For every heart I've hurt
And every soul I've bought.

…But do you know what I hate most of all?

That the girl lost inside those words
never got to see me rise from her fall.

And I'll be damned to rise from her fall just
to let her dive back into my darkness and
die.
For I am her
And she is me.

Together we rise.

Hand in hand.

Fighting off the tide

Inside my mind As

one.

My Roadmap to Recovery

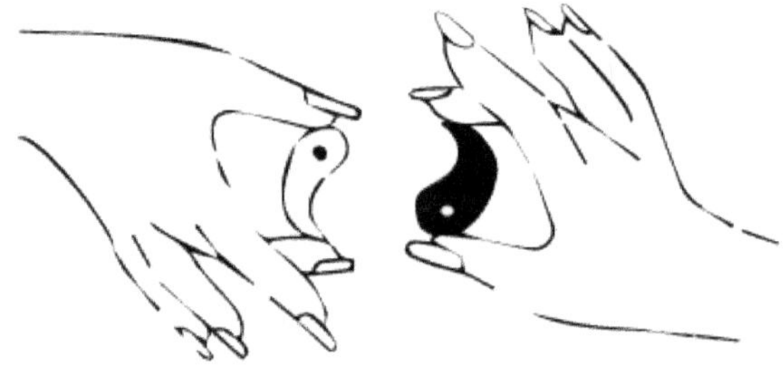

The white scars on my skin
Remind me of all the places I have been.

The people I've met and tears that were shed;
These white scars remind me of the girl that is
dead.

They are the grass that grows on top of her
grave;
For six feet under is where she will stay.

Finally I see

The valley of
Death

Finally grew into

The valley of
Life

When I broke
My shattered soul free

From everything
I knew you to be.

Hues of Hope

Strokes of gray
Smeared across golden blue skies

Shielding the sun
As it begins to rise

Protecting its light
From the darkness of this life.

But soon the clouds Will
dissolve into the sky

Leaving the sun alone to shine.

God… Isn't that what is beautiful about it all?

That even as the clouds

Try to protect the sun—
The lifeline to all breathing beings

She will still shine her light.
Because she will always endure the fight.

She will always rise

Just to help us
Stay alive.

Message in a Bottle

Note to self:

I will no longer sacrifice
The pleasures of life

To become
Who you wanted me to be.

Instead,

I will become
What I want.

I will become
Who I need.

I will become...

Sincerely,
Me.

www.ingramcontent.com/pod-product-compliance
Lightning Source LLC
LaVergne TN
LVHW010932200726
843509LV00013B/2180